The Respect They Deserve...

Isn't about time we gave the respect back to our native insects, their environments, and homes?

For well over two hundred years our insects have been in their personal fight to survive. They don't have a voice, they cannot shout, scream, and make a noise when their homes are destroyed, the only sign they give, is when they no longer exist...!

The emphasis for the 2023 Chelsea Flower Show was on native fields and meadow flowers and grasses, and how refreshing to see the abundance of differently coloured flowers, their shape, form, texture, and vibrancy; some petals glistened as the rays of sunshine caught their movement in the soft spring breeze, and what a treat for any human being to enjoy the moments of this year's Chelsea Flower Show...!

They Want to Survive...

The butterfly you see, has many jobs to do, not only the will to survive but to pollenate the flowers it visits but to make babies for next year too…!

Its time spent is only a few, with so many jobs, and soon, this beautiful creature will need to support the new…

So fragile its wings and glorious too, but delicate as fairy dust, and now too often, too few…!

The butterfly has many messages to give, for it is the story, the story to live…!

Like mothers, from nature we find, the will to produce their babies each year, and to do just that, they need to know the earth will be kind…!

For once the babies are new, the mum's job is done, its short life is lived, for its legacy it leaves, its babies for next year, the flowers it pollinates and the beauty it gives…!

When you see your next butterfly, please take the time to ponder, and then wonder, not only at the joy of the sight, but at the work it does with all its might….!

Welcome to Part Three –

'The Magic of Chelsea' -
A Flower Show Like No Other

We are now into part three of our exciting Chelsea flower journey and what a journey it has been, full of excitement, colour, fun and adventure.

There are not only flower growers and many artists showing their sculptor displays, but there is a myriad of different people from around the world, and these people all bring their uniqueness and ideas to this magical event.

To sit in one of the many restaurants or cafés while eating our egg and cress sandwiches, and sipping a Pimms, one can hear different accents, each full of excitement and enjoyment as the conversations grow louder and the laughter continues.

And so it is, we remember the sunny day, aching and tired feet and the hundreds of photographs, going into the thousand, sifting through the brochures as we recall the event…

And yes, we hope to be there in 2024, the flight tickets booked so the plans are in place….!

If you have purchased this book without its cover, it may be a stolen book.

Neither the publisher or the author is under any obligation to provide professional services in anyway, legal, health or in any form which is related to this book, its contents advice or otherwise.

The law and practices vary from country to country and state to state.

If legal or professional information is required, the purchaser, or the reader should seek the information privately and best suited to their particular needs, and circumstances.

The author and publisher specifically disclaim any liability that may be incurred from the information within this book.

All rights reserved. No part of this book, including the interior design, images, cover design, diagrams, or any intellectual property (IP), icons and photographs may be reproduced or transmitted in any form by any means (electronic, photocopying, recording or otherwise) without the prior permission of the publisher. ©

Copyright© 2023 MSI Australia

All rights reserved.

ISBN: 978-0-6459680-0-2

Published by How2Books
Under licence from MSI Ltd, Australia
Company Registration No: 96963518255
NSW, Australia

See our website: www.how2books.com.au
Or contact by email: sales@how2books.com.au
Covers and Copyright owned by MSI, Australia

MSI acknowledges the author and images, text and photographs used in this book.

10% of the sale of each book helps to support Diabetes Type One and Cancer Research.

Content   Page

Title	Page
Oh, and Then There Were Tulips…!	1
Gladiolus	3
Sunshine and Lilies – Who Could Ask for More…?	5
Dahlia Beach	8
Iris or Flag Iris…?	9
The Iris – Poem	12
The Pleasure of Delphiniums	13
Amazing Maple	15
The Water Garden	16
The Salad Bowl	17
Old Fashioned Violas are Back and in Abundance	18
Shots of Magic	20
Pretty Gardens	21
Different Gardens – Different Approaches to Gardening	25
Different Combinations & Peace of Mind	26
Sweet Peas	27
Who Remembers Wallflowers?	28
Gardens to Capture Dreams	29
Splendid Grasses	30
Bonsai and Perfection	32
Another Reign Begins	35
Garden Accessories	36
The Ancient Art of Pebble Laying	37
Interesting Stalls – The Delphinium Society	38
Susan Entwistle Art	39
Bee The Change	40
Mr Fothergill's	41
Containers Made from Husks	42
The Peony Girl	43
Clothes of the Future	44
Treats of the Show	46
The Reason Why…? The Magic of Chelsea	51
Other Books that May Interest You	52

Oh, and Then There Were Tulips...!

Tulips were originally found in Asia, where they were first cultivated by the people of Turkey as early as twelve hundred years ago.

The origin of the name is also Turkish and originated from the word 'turban'.

Like so many different species of plants, tulips were introduced to Europe in the 16th Century.

They then became popular in the Netherlands, where they are associated to today.

It is not only the colour and shape that attracts people to these popular flowers, but they are also edible, this is unlike the daffodil, which is not edible...!

Tulips are a member of the onion and garlic family, having said that, if eaten, the bulbs may cause gastrointestinal distress, nausea, and vomiting.

Like the bulbs, it is not advisable to eat either the stem or the leaves of the plant.

Tulip petals may be used for garnishing on cupcakes, and, or, on many celebration cakes.

With such displays, not only of single-petal flowers, but those now being introduced in the double or multi-petal varieties.

The above photograph gives a stunning collection of multi-petalled blooms and showcases the advancement in shape, form, and colour these beautiful flowers have become, in the 21st Century. 'Sugar Crystal' the name given to the delightful specimens below, would make perfect wedding or celebration flowers.

Gladiolus

Happy smiles and a delight to speak with the women in the above photograph, who were both from Pheasant Acre Plants. They were informative about their gladiolus plants and the gladiolus on display.

Unfortunately, we could not buy any bulbs as we needed to travel back to Australia, and Australia, like so many countries have strict Border controls for any form of flora, fauna and organic materials coming into the country, and that is understandable!

Just the same, I would have loved to 'buy up big... on the bulbs on offer!

With such splendid and vibrant colours, these blooms were a crowd pleaser to everyone that saw them.

Can you imagine so many colours within one variety of flowers…? And opposite, this beautiful salmon pink, always popular in the flower trade.

I can remember, when I first came to Australia, I made many gladioli roses from this colour.

I still think, if brides want to choose a single wedding flower to carry on their wedding day, there is nothing nicer than a single white gladiolus rose with trailing ivy for simplicity and beauty, they may also be affordable…!

Having said that, there are many floristry techniques that have been lost in the effort to cut costs and to create wedding bouquets quickly and affordably.

Sunshine and Lilies – Who Could Ask for More...?

How majestic these flowers have become; they are used as single flower stems in a bud vase or in great profusion in large hotel foyers. They do not only create a grand entrance but give the feeling of opulence, luxury, and wellbeing.

Not only do they give us visual excitement, but the perfume can send our senses into confusion, almost intoxicating us to the point of feeling 'heady, and happy'…

Harts Nursery had a breath-taking collection of colours and both single and double flowering lilies at this year's show.

My goodness, opposite, who could doubt the beauty of these pretty, pink-edged double flowering lilies? With such a display, they almost suggest they are a little piece of heaven sent to keep us happy and safe in time a of uncertainty as our world and its people go through many imposed and different changes.

From pastel colours to fire and fervour, when seeing such a display, the colours excite and calm the human spirit!

From mass displays to single blooms, all are beautiful specimens of achievement…!

It is a privilege to take these beautiful photographs and to have the honour of being able to speak and write about these magnificent blooms.

Dahlia Beach...

With over 4,000 dahlias for the season planted, Dahlia Beach is in full flow creating a kaleidoscope of colour at Chelsea this year.

From picking your own dahlias, to parties, and flower arranging, all is on offer at the venue of Dahlia Beach.

You can take a picnic, explore the farm, shop, enjoy the lake, or have a coffee at the café, there are no limits to having a fun and enjoyable day.[2]

---

[2] Photographs, courtesy of https://www.dahliabeach.co.uk/pyo-dahlias

Iris Or Flag Iris...?

As a child growing up in England, I can remember iris flowers growing in gardens and on rubbish tips, but those days are long since gone.

The planting of iris in gardens goes back to about 1469 BC at the time of King Thutmose III of ancient Egypt.[3]

The King was an enthusiastic gardener and would covet plants, unlike many kings who would covet gold!

In the conquest of Syria, the King discovered irises growing in great numbers and introduced them into his own garden. The flower soon found influence in Egypt and was much admired by the Egyptian population. Quickly the flower symbolised the renewal of life; the three petals were thought to signify faith, wisdom and valour or great courage.

Over many generations, the iris has provided medicinal remedies and contributed to the perfume industry. It, too, is an ingredient in the making of incense used in religious ceremonies.

[3] Iris: A Brief History // Missouri Environment and Garden News Article // Integrated Pest Management, University of Missouri

Since King Thutmose lll of Egypt BC, the symbol of the iris has been used both in culture and by many monarchs. The fleur-de-lis, now seen as the national emblem of France, the association of the flower and France is thought to come from the three petals of the iris flower. And as we know now, these petals were thought to symbolise faith, wisdom, and valour.

And today, we see this same emblem used in many crowns worn by the monarchy. The symbol also carries through when seen on robes of state and other ceremonial garments.

The iris has been described as a stylised lily, this may be so, but there are so many differences between the iris and the lily in both shape and flower structure!

The history of the iris and our human attachment to this symbolic flower goes back through many generations. Not only do we see the

fleur-de-lis related to the British Monarchy but to the French or Franks as they were then known.

The Franks before conquering Gaul in 486 AD lived for a time, around the river of Lys, in Flanders. The river was bordered with yellow iris flowers, where these flowers still grow today.

Though the flowers around the river are yellow, this is not seen as an iris colour, it is the symbolic shape of the three petals sweeping downwards and the three reaching upwards that has inspired the eternal shape of the much-used fleur-de-lis as national symbols used by both the British and French to date. The symbol is seen on ceremonial occasions, within embroidery into robes or as part of the fine gold and artwork, worked into and through a crown's design.

And so, it is today, the fleur-de-lis is seen on wallpapers, laminated onto clothing, including tee shirts and women's dresses, woven into fabrics including dress fabrics, and woven into carpet and rug designs. The symbol represents tradition, status, and long standing.

Because of the curves in the petal of the iris flower, it makes it a pleasant shape to see and study, therefore, the visual impression becomes a meditative experience.

The Iris

The iris, with petals like the sails of a ship...
standing tall and not wanting to tip....

For when the wind blows, the time will come
when the sails are fragile and old...

Not standing to be seen, magnificent and bold...
The petals of which are significant you see...

For the petals always grow within three...
From knights and king's past, the iris has meant:
Faith, wisdom and valour and a great sign of strength...!

From distant times and up to today
The iris is resplendent in all that I say...

And it is again, my imagination it captures, and words cannot explain...
how my heart lingers through cold winter months
for the sight of this flower and what relief it brings when one is in pain...!

Yes, from the times of the Romans and Greeks, and before
so many, the ancient Egyptians we're told...

This flower has held wonder to their sights as the petals unfold...!

From yellows to whites, purples, and pinks, and to dazzle us,
with beauty, and unable to think...!

For the sails of the ship, that once did we see,
as the season lingers and autumn is near

We know the iris shall soon disappear...

As time does not stand still, it's with heavy heart,
I write these words...

Lingering in thought for the next time I see,
the flower that is perfect and captures my gaze...

Though from a distance, the thoughts are within,
if I look for a while, the iris appears, and a new life begins ...!

The Pleasure of Delphiniums

Delphiniums were in splendour at this year's show and today, we see the outcome of many years of work by delphinium growers. With over 300 species across the world, their beauty and their use in the cut flower industry continues to be developed.

The word delphinium originated from the Greek word delphin, meaning dolphin. The flower's spur resembles the dolphin's back when seen swimming through the water. In Greek mythology, the flowers bloomed from the blood of Ajax, the son of Telamon and cousin of Achilles. He was brave, strong, and played a pivotal role in the Trojan War.

With nearly 40 different colours and over 300 species worldwide, there are many to choose from. It isn't any wonder that we love to see them in our homes, in tall, elegant arrangements for display and event purposes and for show in many flower shops.

'Constance Rivett' is a pure white delphinium with a white eye and makes a superb wedding flower in both wedding bouquets or used in flower displays for decoration at a church or wedding venue.

Delphiniums are part of the Ranunculaceae family which includes buttercups, columbines, and monkshood.

Wild delphinium is found in the Northern hemisphere, and the mountainous ranges of tropical Africa. Delphinium is also known as larkspur. Having worked and owned businesses in the flower industry, to a florist, the words delphinium and larkspur relate to two different tall flower types, both of which are used in commercial floristry.

Despite its beauty and appeal, delphinium is a poisonous plant. After working with the flowers, wash your hands. Delphinium is no different to many plants we decorate our homes or workplaces with; if we want to use their beauty to enhance our lives, we need to understand that their beauty comes about by the genetics they inherit; the genetic makeup of plants is designed to ensure their survival.

In the above, at this year's show, the colours of the delphiniums are enhanced by the accompanying and sharp contrasted begonia flowers.

Amazing Maple...

Acer, commonly known as Maple are believed to have originated in China. They are now dispersed through Asia, Europe, Northern Africa, and parts of the Southern Hemisphere, including Australia.

Recognition of the maple usually relates to the shape of their palmate shaped leaves. Their closest relative being the Horse Chestnut.

Maples have a sweet sugary sap which was used to sweeten foods by the Northern American Indians.

These beautiful trees show their exciting colours during autumn, and the display at this year's show was breathtaking and the colour spectacular.

The Water Garden

Nestled within the Great Pavilion, we were surprised to see this amazing aquatic garden full of different aquatic plants, including some green aquatic grasses, flowering plants, and many different shaped leaf plants all of which add great interest to any pond setting.

The audience too, were enjoying the display. The water was kept in place by 200 x 100mm oak, possibly treated pine or a sustainable material used in the retaining walls which proved to be effective in appearance and structure.

With such a use of materials, it gives us the idea, we can create our water feature gardens in almost any location.

The water was not only calming to see, but the effective use of beautiful plants added to the ambiance of the display.

The Salad Bowl

With such a selection of edible salad greens and assorted herbs on display; it was a remarkable collection of almost designer foods, some of which were organic, and that is always good to know.

Brighter Blooms of Lancashire left 'no stone unturned' when displaying their products for healthy eating and living. It's great to see the turnaround in produce taking place; we are now becoming aware of how good eating relates back to good health and wellbeing.

Old Fashioned Violas are Back and in Abundance...!

What is it about these little treasures that makes your heart happy? Their faces are exquisite, and they show a smile to you every time you look at them.

From lavender to white, a bit of yellow-to lemon here and there and then there is this remarkable display of treasures, with many, held memories from many people's childhoods I should imagine!

Is it any wonder, this display won the 'Silver Gilt Medal' at the Show?

Most violas are found in temperate climates of the Northern Hemisphere, some in Hawaii and in areas within Australia and the Andes.

Some have a sweet perfume, and the scent is part of their enticing appeal.

Violas and violets have been cultivated since ancient times and used for medicinal purposes, perfumes, and colouring. Violets dipped in a sugar solution can be used in decorating cakes, or unsugared may be added to salads and used as ornamental decoration on food dishes.

Shots of Magic

From gasps of pleasure to the excitement of seeing a magnitude of colour in one spot allows the eyes and brain to feast on the sight seen.

Masses of flowers, coloured foliage, the dominant one being Coleus which can be easily grown from a cutting.

Pretty Gardens...

Keeping oneself on track while visiting each garden, taking notes, and photographs, and using all our human senses, we collect the information we need to create this beautiful book.

It is not only our recall we rely on, but the excitement of the day, the visit to the show and our love of the event each year.

Soft colours, soothing greens and the fine foliage shapes all help bring together this amazing collection developed to stimulate the human senses and this it does.

So many of the plants are familiar to my childhood, and I am sure to many of our readers memories.

There was a profusion of colour, shape, and form as we were ready to see the next visual delight.

With soft dancing yellows, touches of orange, lavender and pink colours, and the tiny faces of daisies, all help to bring home to us the importance of protecting our wildflowers, thus allowing our native animals and insects the food they need.

Great news, old fashioned lupins flowers were seen at several stands at the show. Not only are they colourful and make wonderful displays in the garden, but the lupin seed is gaining favour as an alternative food source to soy!

With a greater number of people on the planet to feed, the lupin seed offers many benefits. The seed known as the lupin bean, can be used in different foods, as a flake, or flour. The bean contains a full range of amino acids, contrary to the soybean.

Lupin flour can be made into bread and cake foods. It is high in protein, is naturally gluten-free and low in fat.

Lupins can be grown in temperate climates and are increasingly becoming known as a cash crop for farmers. Our lupins offer many other benefits, once established and in bloom, they offer a bountiful food larder for our pollinating insects, including the bees.

Masses of ground covering orchids including cypripediums of different types and the lily Arisaema Sikokianum, also known as the Japanese Cobra Lily is seen in the below photograph.

Because of the white-on-white colours in the flower, you will notice the dark outer flower reveals the inside white large, swollen sex organ (spadix) of the flower. The spadix provides a deep contrast to the flower when compared to the dark purple petal, (spathe).

The plant grows well in well-drained, dry soil. The plant remains striking until it goes dormant in late summer when it then rests until the next season.

It's an ideal plant for a woodland garden.

Opposite photograph courtesy Wiki Commons.

While I was the appointed florist at the Prime Ministers Lodge, Canberra, Australia, one of the plants growing in the gardens of the Lodge, were the below Solomons Seal. I love this for floral design work.

The natural bend in the plant offers a great opportunity to use the flower stem from the back so that full beauty of the bell-shaped flowers can be seen.

The tiny flowers are hardy and if wired separately, can be used in headdress design and in small wedding bouquets; they are a lot of work, but are a different approach to other flowers more readily used in wedding work.

The last time I worked with these delightful flowers was at the Prime Minister's Lodge, and in flower arrangements for Queen Elizabeth ll's visit on her Australian tour in 1980.

Different Gardens – Different Approaches to Gardening

It appears that clipped lawns and sharp garden edges are becoming ideas of the past, and now we are seeing consideration for animal and insect habitats.

Giving back our gardens to the little creatures that help to keep our gardens and soil healthy is just one small step forward.

It's refreshing to see the emphasis on small but healthy environments, not only for the natural wildlife and environment but also for us humans…!

Understanding that the good environments we each create pays us back in many ways. When our children can grow and play in healthy gardens, we too, feel that benefit.

If we grow our own vegetables in healthy soils, we again feel the benefit.

By taking small steps to create a healthy garden and environment, we will all gain the benefits.

Different Combinations & Peace of Mind...

With layers of different field and wildflowers in our gardens, we too, can enjoy the natural beauty that each season brings.

With changing colours in the seasons to the different textures that help to give us a visual smorgasbord of delight.

Ranunculi to buttercups, and alliums and then to purple iris, all have intrigue and fascination for our senses and good mental health.

Taking the time to look, see, experience and wonder pays dividends in giving us the ability to find peace, tranquillity, and solace within our busy lives.

Sweet Peas

As pretty as they are, the pea of the sweet pea is not good for human consumption. The only living beings to enjoy these pods and their peas are aphids, snails, caterpillars, and some rabbits.

Having said the above, we should enjoy the cultivated and wild sweet peas as they are a truly fragile and beautiful flower.

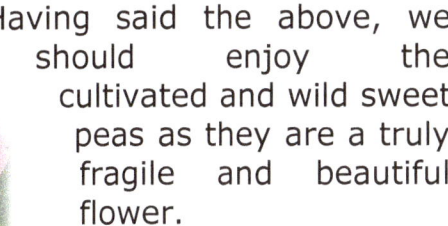

Who Remembers Wallflowers?

The heady fragrance of summer as I played in my grandmother's garden in Sussex in England came rushing back to me as I saw this stand at the show.

It was lovely to see these old-fashioned flowers again, and it seems, there are double blooms now…!

Fresh and clean, the colours and foliage and looking deeply into the bottom photograph, the traditional reddish-brown colour is seen.

In the bottom photograph, you can see is a nice sharp citrus yellow. There may have been more of these delightful flowers, but we were limited for time and the day was long….!

Let's hope, by this first appearance, it's a sign of more to come. It was an absolute treat to see these gems make an appearance.

Gardens to Capture Dreams

How nice is it, to stop and dream? The beautiful displays in the below photographs give us that opportunity, to stop, take a moment and just enjoy.

Each flower, each leaf that grows are all visual gifts for us to enjoy, if we do not see their beauty, that is our missed opportunity that will not come again!

Splendid Grasses

The stand wins Gold, and with so much emphasis on the need to manage and look after our environment, it is not a surprise that grasses have taken a big leap forward with the national awareness of and to global warming.

It is the preservation of what we have and how to enjoy and work with the natural world that is going to keep humankind safe.

This picture-perfect photograph of the grasses on display is one of the reasons it makes a long-haul flight so worthwhile.

Bonsai and Perfection

How many years of dedication does it take to create such magnificent miniature growing trees?

The art of growing small trees goes back to ancient China, and the year, 700 CE. The Chinese were using superior techniques to create dwarf trees in containers.

Originally this artform was only practised by the elite society of China. As the years passed, the Japanese also adopted the ancient art and indeed, the art of Bonsai creation is associated with Japan today. Bonsai are certainly living works of art and greatly admired throughout the world.

Bonsai is the Japanese word, meaning, 'tree in a pot'. The miniature trees are grown and have the representation of nature.

Depending on the culture associated to the creator of the tree, the tree represents and symbolises, harmony, patience, in some instances, luck, and balance.

In some religions, the bonsai represents meditation and contemplation.

The fascination of early explorers in ancient China when discovering miniature trees with their stunted and gnarled trunks in high alpine areas may have been the start of this art form. Taoist Monks, as early as the 4th Century BCE believed in recreating nature. Many people may have also believed the shapes may contain magical properties.

The art of bonsai is also recreated in many painted artworks on porcelain, in pictures, on fabrics and other impressions where the bonsai image is used.

There is also a connection to, and within human thinking, to the bonsai shaping of tree branches, many animal impressions and in yoga positions. Accordingly, the first pictorial indication of creative tree miniaturisation was found in 706 CE in the tomb of Prince Zhang Huai.

Within this article, we can only feature some of the amazing bonsai on display. As can be seen, small flowering trees can also be trained into stunning shapes and, at the right time of year, come into flower.

There are many trees that can be made into bonsai, here are some: Crepe Myrtle, Hibiscus, Apple, Maple, Azalea, Bougainvillea, Cape Honeysuckle, Cherry, Pomegranate and Wisteria.

With an interest in creating wellbeing in our lifestyles, the hobby of creating bonsai would support the knowledge, identifying the stillness of the mind, the quiet meditation of self, and the deep and satisfying experience of watching a living tree grow into its natural and beautiful shape.

Of course, if a seasonal tree was chosen, such as maple, there would also be the natural and seasonal changes that would take place giving added colour and enjoyment to the experience…!

Another Reign Begins...

In last year's book, we saw this amazing impression of her late Majesty, Queen Elizabeth ll, by Ming Veevers Carter. It was an incredible capture, created through clever flower placements, of the image of the late Queen.

The photograph was shot in the late afternoon, hence the light in the background.

This year, the Scottish Plants Company, Binny, has created the intricate crown image below for the new Monarch, King Charles lll.

The intricate bringing together of stripped vine and branches are woven into different parts of the crown creating different textures within the shape.

When comparing the size of the creation with the gentleman in the photograph, it brings home the size and volume of the design.

It is indeed a study and there needs to be time to appreciate the work undertaken to create such a masterpiece.

Garden Accessories

The Ornate Garden Company displayed some of its designs at the show. From designs that go from completely round spheres to offset and oval shapes.

These small, but separate rooms could have many uses in the garden, from an extra reading room and small library, to adding a small and separate dining room, the only limitation in its use is thinking, 'how can I make use of this delightful added addition to our garden?'

The opposite interior shows the pretty and positive contribution such an outside addition can make to any garden or outside setting. One of the suggestions made was to add an outside business, office, or study area, while another was to make such a room into a small nursery if a person is wanting to start a business.

Depending on personal requirements, this simple idea could be adapted to meet many family or individual needs. Please keep in mind Council Planning.

The Ancient Art of Pebble Laying

The ancient art of pebble laying goes back thousands of years. This art was mainly kept for use on pavements and seen firstly in the Eastern Mediterranean areas. From the Mediterranean to Asia Minor where this artform has been seen on excavated floors from the 7th and 8th centuries BC.

By looking at the top photograph, one is drawn to the intricate use of shadowing by grading the pebbles in different tonal values.

It was incredible to see this art in revival and with such detailed images, one, the image of a flying bee in the distant, opposite photograph. With such details, in the produced work, and all created by grading the pebbles by colour and shape.

These are not only remarkable pieces of skilled artwork, but so appropriate in this time of global awareness to the plight of our insects but in the use of collected pebbles, from their natural environment that gives pleasure to all who have the good fortune to see the images.

Interesting Stalls
The Delphinium Society

We have written on the delphinium plant and its flowers earlier in the book. Having said that, the Delphinium Society, by its creation of the pretty stall is worth a mention here.

By the attractive and novel approach of a shop front, the Delphinium Society have created the feeling of, 'I want to enter here to see what this is all about…!'

The use of the colours of lovely English garden in mid-summer was beautiful to see.

Susan Entwistle Art

Susan Entwistle

The superb use of vibrant colours in, not only the artwork of the paintings, but by utilising the art in the making of other products such as cushions, gift cards, baubles, and other forms of gifts, makes Susan's artwork multi-purposed.

The original paintings are beautiful. Susan captures the scenes in the, pointlist style of modernism, which makes her work extraordinary. Susan seizes the colourful combinations of the seasons, which, in turn, captures the imagination and is completely playful on the mind.

When looking at the paintings, it's difficult not to smile, to feel happy and the sunshine of the moment.

Bee The Change

Caring for our bees and insects must be a priority as we move more into the global awareness, that the planet is under threat.

A Scottish Charity Foundation, 'Bee The Change', and within the heading, the Bumblebee Conservation Trust, is helping to raise awareness about the plight of the bumblebee and the need to protect its habitat.

In the spring, the bumblebee queens appear from hibernation and start to look for a safe home that is dry, sheltered, and safe where she can raise her young. As humans create more building sites, fewer nesting sites become less available. These bees do an amazing job in fertilising wildflowers, and crops, therefore, they need our help. For more information and the website, please see below.[4]

[4] Homepage - Bee The Change | Bumblebee Conservation Trust

Mr Fothergill's...

Mr Fothergill's offers flower and vegetable seed ranges in partnership with the RHS. Mr Fothergill's has grown from humble beginnings to become one of the biggest European suppliers of seed to the hobby garden market ...

An extraordinary stall, with old-world charm....

Containers Made from Husks

The sooner, we the consumers, are not using plastics, we all know, our planet will be in a much better place!

With remnants of the Industrial Revolution and the great move forward into using synthetics in clothing, furniture, children's toys, household goods, food, and drink containers to mention only a few, it is a relief to see the food husk being re-cycled into usable objects.

The company 'Husk' creates usable house and kitchen utensils and containers, cookware and tableware from the biodegradable agricultural bi-product waste that are eco-friendly and plastic free.

With the few items seen in the above photograph, we can see just how versatile the husk can be if used in everyday home items. That may just be the starting point, as a mum and grandmother, it would be great for me to see children's toys made of something other than plastic…!

The Peony Girl

'Fun and carefree...' is how the Peony Girl describes her artwork. With so many beautiful paintings to see, which are truly wonderful, it would be difficult to not see the smiles the work brings to its viewers.

Siyuan, pronounced 'see you anne', loves peony flowers and has spent her life in China, Europe, including the Netherlands and Britain.

She enjoys the challenges her work brings to her. From trying new techniques, some of which work, some do not, each offer Siyuan a new opportunity to learn about her art. She doesn't let the challenge deter her and often works with a difficult task to make it work for her. In the process, she creates different and beautiful paintings of the peony flower.

The peony flower is not only a beautiful flower but is regarded as the national flower of China.

Clothes of the Future

Clothes made from roots of plants in the future cannot be ruled out.

From the photographer and artist, Zena Holloway, we have a great alternative to fabrics made from synthetic materials. Zena grows grass roots, which are environmentally friendly, to make her fabric.

These fabrics are a great leap forward and have many advantages for the textile industries and the world of fashion.

When looking at the above dress design, it is easy to see how this material can so easily fit into the fashion industry.

Taking the idea even further, such fabrics could be made for the higher end of the fashion industry, including wedding and evening gowns. Once developed, such a material could be used in everyday clothing.

When we stop to think about the ancient Egyptians and their use of flax to create their linen clothing, it gives us multiple ideas. Linen is a fabric that allows the body to naturally breathe, is cool to wear, and has hard wearing benefits. Fabrics made from natural root would also offer this human benefit of body comfort.

For different ideas to fashion, we have included the above photograph, which may allow the synthetic textile industry to re-invent itself![5]

---

[5] Photograph, courtesy ZenHolloway.com

With such amazing ideas and creations coming from Zena Holloway, the artist, maker, and material innovator, it is remarkable to see how roots, which grow all over the world, can be used in textile production.

It is not only the use of the root in clothing, but the world population benefits with such ideas, and this can be a great advantage to us all.

Remarkable clothing designs, which can be used in so many ways, are inventive and forward thinking put into action to create the outcome which you see in these photographs.

Treats of the Show

With each show exhibit there were visual surprises in store. In the photographs in this section, we are introducing some delightful flower exhibits that can truly stand alone.

Not greatly used in the flower industry, this beautiful plant and its flowers offer versatility, lasting strength, and a variety of colours from white, to different blues and now there is 'Agapanthus Blackjack', as seen in the photograph opposite.

With all tones of purples being highly popular with brides, will this flower and its colour become a 'must have' for future wedding flowers?

Blackjack has large heads with purple striped blooms.

The plant is recommended for borders and use in containers, the flower industry should not be forgotten as the colour will add a great dimension to the florist when they suggest the use of this flower and its colour…!

Above, this delightful sunflower with its inner golden glow at the base of the petals is just one exhibit. It was in itself, a showstopper.

Above the delightful pink of the Hydrangea serrata, (Euphoria Pink), was the second and runner up, in Plant of the Year exhibits. With a foliage that flushes pink, white, and green and two-toned flowers of white to a hot ruby and pale centres, it was exquisite.

Then, there were the rose exhibits, such delicate colours and displays, they did indeed allow the mind to take a rest, mellow until the next delightful exhibit was seen.

And then below, we see the European Peony flower, and what a spectacle it was to see...?

Soft petals to equal the wings of a butterfly with warm and inviting centre pieces of invitations to insects to come and feast and fertilize while the flower shows off its fragile beauty to all who take the time to stop and look...!

An absolute delight and privilege to see such beautiful flower specimens.

Opposite, 'Californian Poppies' are an old-fashioned garden plant often seen in many gardens in Britain and Europe during the summer months.

Despite its long acquaintance to, the flower gardens, upon its arrival in and when it shows its flowers, it's always a time of sunshine, long, warm evenings and a time of enjoyment in the British and European gardens.

The Californian Poppy was originally native to Northern California and Southern Mexico but is now grown in many other parts of the world. It is a member of the Ranunculus family and is greatly prized by the Native Americans for its medicinal value.

Opposite, the plant 'Dame's Rocket', or Mother of the Evening, or Sweet Rocket or Wild Phlox is a sweet, scented plant that releases a wonderful perfume on summer evenings.

When walking past this plant and if brushed by clothing, the perfume seems to intensify; it can leave lasting and good memories of summer…!

Opposite, this large-leaved lupin grows to about 50-100cm. In flower it attracts many pollinating insects, including bees.

The lupin is used in many informal, cottage gardens where the true grandeur of the flower columns can be seen and show off.

Covering a range of different colours from the deep reds to apricots, pinks, and a range of blues, they are an ideal summer flower, however, they are considered invasive in some countries and regions of the world.

Below, the ivy geranium is always a great asset in any garden whether grown in the garden or flowerpot; they are hardy and seem to withstand tough forgetting to water!

When loved, they show their appreciation by giving us a spectacular display of lasting and colourful flowers; they are very forgiving plants…!

The Reason Why…?
The Magic of Chelsea

Thank you for the wonderful conversations, friendship, and fun we experienced on our one short day during our visit to the United Kingdom.

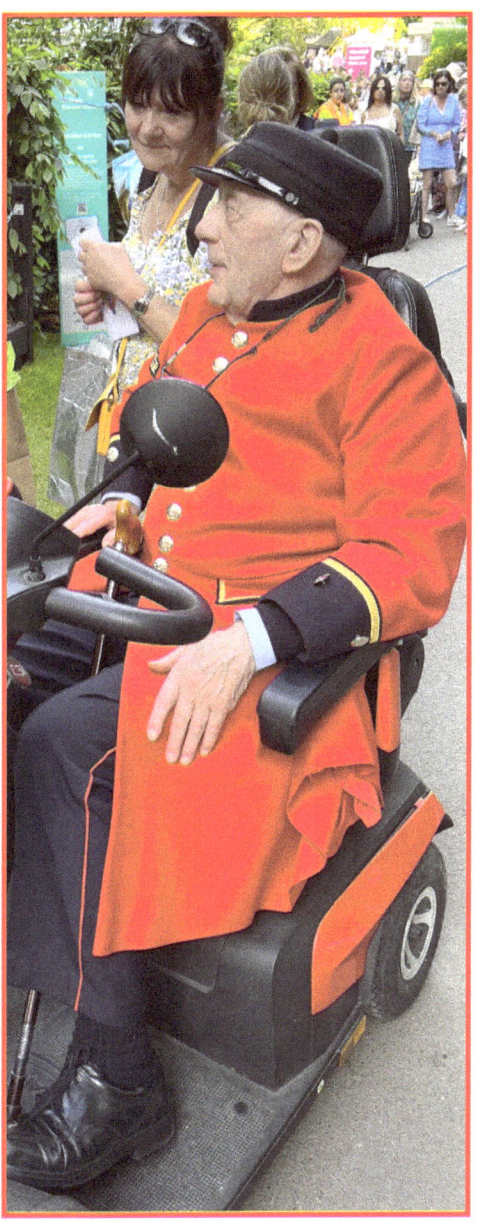

Emblem, Courtesy, The Royal Hospital Chelsea, Home of the Chelsea Pensioners.

Other Books That May Interest You
Available Online
www.how2books.com.au

The book, 'How To Create Easy Wedding Bouquets', introduces you to many techniques in wedding bouquet construction, the different methods used to wire different flowers and leaves, how to tape, ribboning the wedding bouquet handle, how to make a corsage, buttonhole and other industry techniques that will start you on a floristry career.

Our education company, Full Potential Education And Training has been developed to support people who want to learn how to build skills for the floristry industry. The course is a CPD Accredited 20-week online course in commercial floristry wedding bouquet making. It has been designed to support people who want to work for themselves and start a business or for those people who want a trade career in the floristry industry. For more information, please email, admin@fullpotentialtraining.com.au

The book, 'How To Create Easy Flower Arrangements', is an introduction to floral art and commercial floristry in flower arranging. The book is designed to help those people who want to learn flower arranging and construction techniques and will give the foundation knowledge to those people who want to work in the floristry industry.

It will also help people who want to learn flower arranging for pleasure and gift giving, and those people who create flower arrangements for special occasions.

The Magic of Chelsea, 2022, is full of information covering the Chelsea Flower Show, floristry, art and design, sculpture, different plants and how they are used and has other informative and relevant information that gives the reader different information about the topics included. It would be an ideal book for florists, garden centres, nurseries and like businesses to have as a book for sale in their business. For wholesale information, please email: admin@booksforreadingonline.com

Because we love the books we create, and poetry is a big part of the work we do, we could not help ourselves but include this book of different poetry.

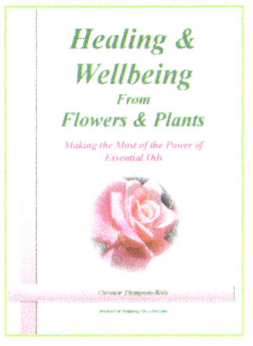
Without plants, we cannot survive. As all flower and lovers know, many plants and trees are under threat! Plants not only help to keep our planet and wildlife healthy, but they also add to our human wellbeing.

This book outlines the benefits of using herbs in our everyday lives. It is colourful and gives a breakdown of herb uses.

All the books are available at
www.how2books.com.au
This book is brought to you from the publishers of:

ISBN: 978-0-6457284-7-7